Something Seems Fishy

John R. Mitchell

with contributions by Gary S. Stanford

"Fish stories told here…. some might be true!"

Copyright 2022 by John R. Mitchell

IngramSpark Publishing

In memory of the loved ones we have lost:
Roy, Juanita and James Mitchell
Robert Mitchell
Phillip McCaffery
Stanley (Lewis) Ritter
Milton and Cleo Stanford
Paul Crosley

This book is dedicated to all our fishing friends, especially Richard Cance, who helped me catch my first Northern Pike, Bill Goatcher, who introduced me to salt water fishing, and Kevin Ballard, who mentored me on catching steelhead.

"Early to bed...early to rise...fish all day...make up lies." Author Unknown

Introduction

Being born and raised off and on in the great state of Wisconsin, you are not a good Badger if you don't hunt and fish. I was introduced to fishing by my father at an early age. We lived on a dairy farm in the central part of the state, and had numerous lakes and rivers not too far from our home. The first farm my father owned had a river running through our property. My Dad was a school teacher in addition to dairy farming, so he had tremendous demands made upon his time. I did get a chance now and then to wet a worm, however.

This is a collection of stories, mostly true (I'm a fisherman; you can trust me) from my past experiences chasing those cold-blooded creatures with fins and tails, and with some contributions from my friend, Gary S. Stanford, also a fisherman of sorts.

"The two best times to fish is when it's rainin' and when it ain't." Author Unknown

"...of all the liars among mankind, the fisherman is the most trustworthy." ~William Sherwood Fox, *Silken Lines and Silver Hooks*, 1954

My first biggest fish

One of my earliest memories is when my father took me fishing at Hamilton Falls, a small waterfall on the north fork of the Wolf River south of our farm in Stanley, Wisconsin.

He took me out on a big flat rock at the base of the falls, baited my hook, and tossed bait and bobber into a pool of water just below the falls. He handed me the cane pole and told me to call out if I needed help. He told me this was a likely place to catch some rock bass, figuring that as a six- year old, I should be able to handle them without his help. The average rock bass is between 6 and 10 in. long, and they rarely weigh over a pound. Dad went a short distance away above the falls, which were about 5 feet high. He was hoping to catch some trout or bass. He had me in his sights, and he figured I was safe.

I watched my bobber dance around in the pool for a while, and all of a sudden it disappeared under the water. Dad had taught me to pull up on the pole when this happened. I did! But something pulled back, and it was bigger than a rock bass. I struggled with the fish for a few moments, but soon I called out for Dad to come and help. I was afraid it would pull me into the river!

He was there quickly and helped me drag a huge fish onto the flat rock. At least to me, it was huge!

"That isn't a rock bass!" I stated.

Dad said it was a redhorse, which is a bottom-feeding sucker related to carp and black suckers, but they live in clear fresh water. Dad unhooked it and measured it.

"Sixteen inches! That's quite a fish."

I was grinning from ear to ear. This was the biggest fish I had ever seen, and **I** had caught it; much larger than the bluegill or sunfish I had previously caught.

Dad put it in a bucket he had brought along, baited my hook, and helped me get my bait back into the water. He said that redhorse were very bony, but good to eat.

He went back to where he was fishing.

Again, I watched my bobber wander around the pool with the current for a time. My attention span was short, and I began watching a pair of mallard ducks downstream. When I looked again to my bobber, it was gone. I had another fish on, and it was another big one.

"Daddy, I need some help again!" I called.

My father was there in a jiffy, and helped me drag another redhorse up onto the rock.

"Johnny, this fish is seventeen inches long," he said. Once again, I was all smiles. My day of fishing was great so far.

Dad baited my hook once more, tossed it into the river, and handed me the pole again.

"See if you can catch another one," he laughed as he went back upstream.

I watched my bobber closely for what seemed like an eternity. I pulled it up when it looked like it went under, but it must have been the current in the stream. The worm hadn't been touched. I dropped it back into the water.

I did this several times. No bites! No fish! Where were they?

Then, bang! The bobber went down and stayed down! I pulled up and had my third fish on the line. The cane pole arched again as I tried to pull it in. I needed help from my father once more!

"Daddy, can you help me? I got another one!"

My father hurried to my side, laughing as he arrived. We pulled a third redhorse up onto the rock. After taking it off the hook, Dad measured it and then chuckled as he looked at me.

"This fish is eighteen inches long. You have done very well today!"

We fished for another thirty minutes or so, but then we had to go home so Dad could milk the cows. He hadn't caught anything, but I brought 3 fish home to brag about to Mom. I felt like I was on top of the world. She fried them the following night for supper, and they tasted great to this mighty six year old fisherman!

"Reading about baseball is a lot more interesting than reading about chess, but you have to wonder: Don't any of these guys ever go fishing?" Author Unknown

My earliest fishing memories

My first memories of fishing was when I was four or five years old. My mother took me to great uncle Lee's and great aunt Hilda's home near us. They had a small river that ran through their property behind their house, and Aunt Hilda set me up with a cane pole to use. We dug some worms for bait in her garden, and soon set out for the nearest bank of the river. Mom baited my hook, and Aunt Hilda explained how to watch my bobber for any fish that might be hungry. Soon, she yelled for me to pull up on my pole, as a fish had taken the bobber under the water. I obeyed, and discovered, to my surprise, that I had a fish dangling from my line.

"That's a nice one," Aunt Hilda exclaimed.

She smoothly removed the fish from the hook, dropped it into a bucket of water she had brought along, and rebaited my hook.

"See if you can catch another one," she cried as I awkwardly dropped the hook, line and sinker back into the water.

Soon, I had another fish to dump into the bucket. Aunt Hilda and Mom were catching fish also, and after a time, Aunt Hilda said it was time to go clean them so she could fry them for supper.

We walked back to the house, and Uncle Lee got the duty of cleaning the fish while Aunt Hilda and Mom cleaned me up and prepared supper.

I recall that the fish we caught that day were shiners, Horned Dace, a few perch and some rock bass. I don't remember how they tasted, but I learned a lifelong skill that afternoon of fishing and enjoying the pursuit of those sometimes wily creatures. Thank you, Aunt Hilda and Mom, for getting this fisherman started.

My biggest fish that DID get away (many years later)

My wife Leslie's sister, Debbie, moved to Florida after she was married to her husband Bill, and for years we had a great place for a vacation; Clearwater, Florida.

We were there one summer, and on a day that both Bill and Deb had to work, Leslie and I headed for a beach close by in the Gulf of Mexico. Leslie planned to do some sunning and wading in the water, and I, of course, planned to fish. I took my spinning rod and tackle box with me, we picked up some shrimp for bait, and we headed to a secluded beach in a nice cove. Florida was hot that day, so we slathered our arms, legs, neck, and all other exposed flesh we could think of with sun screen and then walked from the parking lot down a long trail to a small beach. We were the only ones there; the local residents considered it too hot and remained inside in the air conditioning.

We removed our shoes and socks and waded into the water from the white sandy beach for a time. I got out my fishing rod and began my attempt at finding one of those the elusive finned critters. Bill had said this was a good spot for flounder, and that is what I was hoping for. I had a taste for a good flounder dinner.

I fished in the little cove for a time and soon had a fish take my bait. I fought it for a while and finally pulled in my first flounder. I was amazed at the nasty teeth they had as I extracted my hook and put the fish in a bucket.

A short time later, I had another bite! This time, whatever hit my bait headed for Cuba. Snap! went my spinning rod, and then my line as he headed south. With a broken fishing rod, my fishing time was over, but I could brag about "the big one that got away."

I packed up my fishing gear, and we played on the beach and in the water for a couple of hours until we figured it was time for Bill and Deb to be home from work. We slipped on our shoes and headed to our car.

When we arrived at their house, we discussed my lost fish. Bill thought it might have been a ray, as they are difficult to catch because of how they are built.

About that time, Leslie and I realized the tops of our feet were hurting and, after taking off our shoes, we saw that our feet were badly sunburned. We had neglected to put sun screen on our feet!

For the next several days, we were in constant pain from our bright red feet. We tried various cremes, but the burn would not go away. We learned to pay closer attention to our feet in the future. And, to make matters worse, I didn't get my flounder dinner! But, I did have a fish story to tell.

"I fish because the voice in my head tells me to."
Author Unknown

Fishing with Bill

Another summer vacation found us in Florida once again. Brother-in-law Bill had a fishing boat and I had talked him into taking me fishing while we were visiting. A friend of his at work had suggested we go over to Tampa Bay after dark, motor out under the bridge where Interstate 275 crossed the inlet and we could fish there. The lights from the bridge attracted all types of fish.

We purchased some bait, trailered to a public access to the bay, and launched his boat. Bill's coworker was right; plenty of light, and plenty of fish. I didn't have my baited hook in the water 20 seconds and I had a fish on. When I got it into the boat, Bill identified it as a ladyfish, also known as a bonefish. It was a long, slender silver fish about 18 inches in length with plenty of teeth.

"Are they good eating?" I asked.

"No. Too many bones. Fun to catch, but no good to eat."

I took it off the hook and returned it to the salty water. Within seconds of my bait hitting the water I had another fish on. The ladyfish jumped and fought and, just as Bill had been told, were great fun to catch.

We fished for a couple hours and caught dozens of ladyfish. They cooperated so well that I even caught two with a bare hook. They were all between 15 and 22 inches long. I was actually getting tired of catching fish by the time we decided to head home.

We also caught several small sheepshead and grunt, but Bill didn't think they were edible, so they all went back into the bay. On the way to the house, he admitted he didn't know much about saltwater fish, as he normally went bass fishing in a nearby freshwater lake. He found out the next day that these other fish we had caught were very good to eat.

Before we visited Florida the following summer,

I bought a book on saltwater fishing and read up on all the fish we might find in Florida's gulf waters, but I sadly discovered when we arrived that Bill had sold his boat. Oh, well!

"The charm of fishing is that it is the pursuit of that which is elusive but attainable, a perpetual series of occasions for hope." Author Unknown

Four guys from Chicago

Although I didn't experience this story and I cannot verify it as being true, I include it here for your enjoyment.

A family friend named Phillip took me fishing one summer at a lake in central Wisconsin, not far from his home. We were nearing our destination when he pulled into the parking lot of a small store. A big sign advertised "Bert's Bait Shop."

"We are stopping to see Bert," he said. "Bert runs this shop and is one of the most honest bait shop owners I've ever met. He will tell you where to fish, what's biting, what's not, and which bait to use. Some bait shop operators will tell you anything to sell bait, but not Bert. You can trust him."

We walked into the bait shop and Bert greeted Phillip by name.

"What's biting, Bert?"

"Not much, Phil. You might find a few perch on

Mud Lake around the lily pads, but not until later in the afternoon. Nothing else is biting at all. Who's your friend?"

Bert was an older man, shorter than me and heavy set, with grey hair cut short and a Green Bay Packers cap covering a receding hairline. He wore a black Leinenkugel's Beer t-shirt and blue jeans held up with suspenders. Phillip introduced me and told Bert I had come north from Indiana to visit and perhaps catch a few fish. When Bert found out I lived close to Chicago, Illinois, he began to laugh.

"I got a story to tell you boys about four guys from Chicago," he stated.

"A couple of summers ago, these four young fellas came in to my shop. It was mid-summer, and nothin' was bitin', like now. They had driven all night from Chicago, and were here for a long weekend. It was Saturday morning, and they had to be home Tuesday night. They were staying at a campground over yonder. I sold them some crappie minnows and suggested they try Nice Lake over by Birchwood. They thanked me and left with their minnows, red worms and some crickets.

"Next morning they were back. 'Nothin' bitin',' they said. I suggested they try Balsam Lake, down the road from where they had been yesterday. They took some more minnows and crickets with them.

"Monday morning they were in again. No luck so far. I had heard from some other fisherman that they had caught a couple bass on Sand Lake, a little to the north. Off they went with more minnows, and some leeches.

"Tuesday morning they were here as soon as I opened.

"'Look, Bert, we promised our friends back home a fish fry when we got back, but so far we got nothin'. We need to be on the road home by 3:00 today. What do you suggest?'

"'Well, you might try Lake Chetek. Maybe you might wake up a northern pike or two.'

"I sold them some larger minnows for pike, but as I was filling their bucket, one of the guys pointed to another tank and says, 'What do you have in here?'

"He was lookin' at a tank with some black suckers I sold for muskellunge bait. 'Them are black suckers. You don't want them. They's for muskie. You gotta be one heck of a good fisherman to catch one of them!'

"These fish were a good twelve inches long. The guy had some kind of smart idea, and asked me to take a dozen of them, clean 'em and then wrap and freeze 'em for me. They would be back by 3:00 to pick 'em up. I wasn't sure what they would do with black suckers, but I sold 'em the fish.

"They headed out with their pike minnows, and I proceeded to clean and freeze a dozen black suckers.

"Promptly at 3:00 they came by and picked up their package of fish. I asked what they were going to do with them.

"'Well, we promised our friends a walleye fish fry, and these are the biggest fish we could find. We'll use these.'

"That next summer they were back for another weekend of fishin'. I remembered them as the guys from Chicago and asked about their fish fry.

"'We fried up those black suckers, and told our friends they were walleye. Our friends told us they were the tastiest walleye they had ever eaten.'"

We didn't catch any fish on our trip, but we also didn't take home any black suckers under the pretense they were walleye, trout or even lake perch....

Incidently, Phillip professed to be a Muskie fisherman himself. He had never caught one, but he fished for them frequently. He had some gigantic lures to prove it.

"Fishing is fun…catching is better." Author Unknown

Another fish story with Phillip

A number of summers after I moved to Indiana, I made trips north to visit relatives and friends in Wisconsin, and I always had hopes of going fishing during my visits.

On these trips north, I always stopped to visit our friends, Hazel and Phillip. Phil had been a classmate with my father's in high school, and he and Hazel remained friends with us forever. This year, he volunteered to take me up to Brown Lake, a few miles north of Phillip's home town. He gathered up his fishing gear, and showed me what looked like a very short baseball bat.

"What's this for?" I asked. "How big are these fish? Do we need this to beat them over the head?"

"That's for your bait."

"I've never had to club worms or minnows before."

"No, no! This is for catching different bait. You'll

understand in about 20 minutes."

We headed north, and Phil guided me onto a dirt side road that lead into a very swampy area.

"There should be plenty of frogs here," he said as he pulled out a minnow bucket and two clubs. "When you find a frog, club him and stick him into the minnow bucket. I put a couple inches of water in this to keep the frogs wet. When we get to the lake, I'll show you how to hook them up for bass. Black bass love frogs."

He was right about there being plenty of frogs; the difficulty was reaching them with these short clubs in a swamp without getting wet. I managed to smack four frogs and dropped them into the bucket. Phil had six he had batted into submission.

We drove a few miles further north and found another dirt road leading to Brown Lake. There was a small parking area there, and Phillip showed me how to hook a frog onto a spinner so when casting, it looked like it was swimming. I found a spot on the lake between two trees and began casting and reeling in my frog. On the third cast, something hit the bait, but let go.

I cast the frog back to where it had been hit, and I got a second hit, but no fish. I looked the frog over to see if I had put him on the hook properly, and noticed teeth marks in the skin of his legs. Whatever was striking the frog wasn't hitting it high enough to get the hook.

I had an idea on how to solve this problem. Going through my tackle box, I found some very small hooks on short leaders which I affixed into the feet, and attached them to the spinner. Now, whatever hit the legs of the frog should find a hook in its mouth.

On my third cast, something hit the frog. It also got

a hook! I had a fish on.

It put up quite a fight, but I got it into shore. When I pulled the fish out of the water, I saw that it was a large bullhead. (A bullhead is a relative of the catfish, except they don't get as large.)

I shouted to Phil as I reeled in my fish, and he had come over to see my bass. When he saw the bullhead, he about fell over.

"I can't imagine catching a bullhead on a frog spinner!" he roared. "I can't believe I'm seeing this!'

I took it off the hook and put it into the bucket with the frogs. We fished for several hours with nary a bass showing up.

When it was time to go, the bullhead was still among the living, so I decided to release it back to the lake, along with the frogs. Once we were in the car, Phil laughed all the way home.

"Wait 'til I tell my sons about this," he exclaimed. "They will never believe it. Catching a bullhead with a frog spinner! Har! Har!"

Phil remembered this incident for years afterward, and the bullhead got larger each time he told the story.

"If I fished only to capture fish, my fishing trips would have ended long ago." Zane Grey

A canoe fishing story

After I completed my tour of the world with the U.S. Air Force (Texas, Illinois, Vietnam, The Philippines, Australia and Indiana), I purchased a 19 foot canoe to pursue my fishing desires. Three friends of mine, George, his cousin Will, and Larry went on a fishing trip to Wisconsin with me for a few days that summer. We left Indiana after I got off work on a Friday evening. George had a pop-up camper, and we strapped my canoe to the top of his car and we headed around Chicago into the wilds of northern Wisconsin. We pulled into the Chippewa Falls area around 6:00 a.m. for breakfast at a local restaurant. Two hours later, we arrived at a public (and free) primitive camping area at Long Lake. We popped up the tent, pulled out the wings, and slept for about four hours.

After a makeshift lunch, we put the canoe into the water and tried our hand at fishing. We had bought licenses and bait at a gas station before we arrived at the lake.

Long Lake was one of the clearest lakes I had ever seen. We could see bottom deeper than we could reach it with an canoe paddle. The fishing season had opened just days earlier, and we enjoyed the sunshine and nice spring weather as we caught some panfish for dinner.

That evening we decided to retire early, as we had driven all night and had gotten just four hours of sleep. Larry and I slept in one wing, Will in the other, and George had brought an air mattress which he put on the floor of the camper. The temperature was well into the 70's during the day, and the camper, parked in the sun all afternoon, was very warm inside. George decided he would sleep on top of his sheets and, dressed in his skivvies, was soon off into dreamland. The rest of us got into various discussions about trivial matters.

Soon, we noticed that the temperature was

dropping as darkness crept into our domain. Will turned on a lamp, and we continued to talk, laugh and joke. We gradually migrated into our sleeping bags as the temperature continued to drop.

Will began to laugh and pointed to his cousin. George, who was sound asleep and had begun to shiver with the night chill.

"You think we should wake him up?' Larry asked.

"Nah. When he gets cold enough, he'll wake up and cover himself," Will replied.

We continued to laugh at poor George until finally he grabbed some covers and pulled them over his shaking body.

"Cold enough for you, George?" asked Will.

"Nyahhh!" he responded, barely awake. Within seconds, he was snoring again.

"Even if you've been fishing for three hours and haven't gotten anything except poison ivy and sunburn, you're still better off than the worm." Author Unknown

Another canoe fishing story

Another northern Wisconsin vacation trip took me to meet up with a friend from the area, Richard. Richard had a fantastic sense of humor and had taught me how to fish the rivers and streams for northern pike. I had suggested we go to Pike Lake to see if we could catch anything there. I had stopped at my uncle Lew's house the day before, and when I told him my plans, he invited himself along. I called Richard to see if he would mind.

My canoe would hold three comfortably, and four people when needed. He loved the idea. We met Richard at the Pike Lake Resort. It was the only resort on the lake, which made it very easy to find.

Richard had brought a small folding seat for Lew to sit on, and we had picked up some snack foods for lunch. We packed everything into the canoe, put Lew in the center, and glided out on the lake. It was great in the canoe; the lake water was calm and clear, and it was a bright and sunny day. A great day for fishing.

"I have a fishing story for you," Lew said. "This lake brings back some old memories.

"Shortly after I married my wife, Dorothy, we came up to Pike Lake. I was fishing, and Dorothy was just enjoying the day in our row boat. We were way out on this lake and a sudden storm came up. The wind picked up, the lake started churning, and it started raining. We were headed toward the dock. Dorothy was sitting in the stern of the boat and I was rowing as hard as I could into the wind. We started to see lightning and the rain became a downpour. Dorothy began getting scared and excited. She is a high-strung German and gets worked up and flustered easily.

"Well, the storm was really getting to her and, for some reason, she stood up in the boat. I don't know why she did that, but she started yelling at me to row faster.

"I was doing my best, and was afraid she was going to fall out of the boat, or capsize us, and so I yelled at her. 'Sit down, Dorothy, or I'll hit you with an oar!'

"She looked at me with a very shocked expression, sat down, and was quiet the rest of the way into the dock.

"I don't ever remember yelling at her before then, and very few times since. But she quieted down and let me do my job of getting us to safety."

Richard had brought some minnows from his father's milk cooling tank (that's where he kept his fishing bait) and once we got into a quiet cove, we baited our hooks and began our wait for the pike.

There was no interest in the minnows for quite a while, and we tried several locations around the lake with no results. Suddenly, Richard started reeling in his line.

"Got something! And, it's a big one!"

After fighting the fish for some 10 minutes or so, he finally got it up next to the canoe so we could see it. But it wasn't a fish; it was a huge snapping turtle!

Lew saw it as it surfaced and yelled, "Don't you bring that thing into this canoe!"

"Wow, what a catch!" shouted Richard. "This will bring me $15 or $20 at the tavern!"

"If you try to bring him in here, I'm gettin' out!" exclaimed Lew.

Meanwhile, I had the landing net in the water, but realized the turtle was too big. I also had reservations about sharing my canoe with a snapper.

"This isn't going to work," I called. "Any suggestions?"

"When I get him close to the canoe, see if you can grab his tail."

"He's not coming in here!" Lew repeated.

Richard maneuvered the turtle so I could try to grab onto his tail. I made a lunge into the water and got it. As soon as Richard let up on the line, the turtle spit the hook out of his mouth. I had him for a few moments, anyway. He put his hind legs against the canoe, pushed off, and right out of my hand he slipped, free to return to his watery domain.

"Oh, thank goodness," said Lew. "I was afraid you guys were going to make me hold him in my lap!"

Richard decided it was ok that the turtle got away. "He really was too big to take back home," he nodded.

"What would they do with him at the tavern?" I asked.

"They feature turtle soup once a month, when they can get turtles. It's tasty. You should try it."

"I think I'll pass," I replied, after picturing how ugly that snapper was.

We all rinsed our hands in the lake, and Richard broke out the food. He had bread, a can of baked beans, and..... nothing else.

"Looks like I forgot something. I had lunch meat, paper plates, and other fixin's set out and ready to go. Must have lef them on the table at home."

Making the best of the situation, he opened the beans with his worm knife, and made us baked bean sandwiches.

Lew laughed until tears came.

"I've never had bean sandwiches before. Thank God that turtle didn't have me for lunch!"

"Pity the man who can't distinguish between seven inches and twelve, between half a pound and two, and between four and a dozen. We call them politicians, accountants or fishermen."

A fishy limerick

There was a young fisherman named Chad,
who only went fishing for shad.
"It's a bright silver fish
and it's very delish,
but best if fried in butter, by gad."

Two short canoeing stories, without any fish this time

Story number 1

Early on in our marriage, my wife, Leslie, and I worked at our church with the high school students. One of the projects we organized was a canoe trip to Turkey Run State Park. We could rent canoes, they would take us upstream to The Shades State Park, and we would canoe Sugar Creek back to Turkey Run. We put a group together and bought tickets, making arrangements to arrive at Turkey Run early in the morning of the trip. They packed us into a bus and transported us up the creek to begin our journey, rain or shine.

The person in charge of the venture gave us instructions, telling us where the creek ran deep, where it was shallow, and what to watch out for along the way. A couple hundred yards from where we entered the water, there was a sharp bend with some rapids. We were to keep to the left as we entered the rapids, as there was a massive boulder in the water on the right. If we weren't careful here, the rushing water would smash us into this rock and dump the canoe. Two people were to be in each canoe.

The high schoolers started first, and two of them, Mark and Bob, showed us they had prepared some unsinkable containers. In these, they had packed their lunches, soft drinks, and their dry clothes for after the canoe trip. Everyone else had brought dry clothes and left them in their cars, but not Mark and Bob. They insisted everything would go well.

They were in the first or second canoe that shoved off. We were in the last one, so if anyone needed assistance along the way, we were ready to help them.

Things went fine until we got to the bend with the large boulder. Mark and Bob hadn't listened to the instructions, didn't keep to the left, and got washed into the boulder. We didn't see them, but their canoe was wrapped around the huge rock.

We caught up with them about an hour into our voyage. Two other canoes had helped them aboard. They had lost one paddle and broken the other one, and their unsinkable containers, including dry clothing and food, had gone straight to the bottom of the creek when their canoe capsized. No sight of their belongings could be found.

....

Story number 2

Several years earlier, we had gone on this same trip with our college age church group. As I stated earlier, when we made reservations, we went, rain or shine. This particular day, it was misting when we arrived with the canoes at The Shades, and there were storm warning issued for our area. There were ten or twelve in our group, and so we began our journey down the creek.

About a half hour into our day, the rain began in earnest. We were getting soaked, and decided to take refuge on shore under some tall pine trees. But, as the rain kept up, the trees no longer gave us protection. One of our group leaned some canoes vertically against the trees, and we took some shelter under them. But the storm began producing thunder and lightening. We looked at each other, and decided standing under an aluminum canoe among very tall trees in a lightening storm might not be the smartest idea we could come up with.

So, we put the canoes in the water, got into them, and continued down the creek in the rain. Now our goal was to get to Turkey Run as soon as possible so we could get shelter!

Fortunately, our driving rain let up after a time, but we continued down the creek as fast as we could go. We soon came upon one of the shallow parts, where we actually had to get out and walk the canoes down the creek. By now, we were tired, the rain had stopped for the moment, and there was an island of sand and gravel in the middle of the creek. We had brought sandwiches along, so we ate lunch while we rested. We were about ready to get back into the canoes when we realized they were moving. Our island was decreasing in size, as the creek was rising. We latched onto our canoes, got in, and continued downstream with the rising stream. We found few if any shallow places afterwards due to the rising water.

When we arrived at Turkey Run State Park, we

were over two hours earlier than they had expected us. We also found out that we had been under a tornado advisory during our trek; fortunately for us no tornadoes had been spotted.

"Good things come to those who bait. And, remember, "Carpe Diem" does not mean "fish of the day" unless it is on a menu in a restaurant." Author Unknown

A fishy story

Ted and Danny had traveled to Northern Michigan on a fishing trip. Their day on the lake was exceptional, and they caught their limit on walleye. As they began to pull up their anchor, Ted had a brilliant idea.

"Danny, we found the perfect place to fish today, and caught some really nice fish. Why don't we mark this spot so we can find it tomorrow?"

Danny pulled out a black marker and leaned over the side of their rented boat.

"I can mark the side of the boat with a big X. That way we can find this spot again tomorrow!"

He marked the boat just above the waterline.

"There. Now we can find the fish tomorrow. But, now that it is marked, we need to rent this same boat again!"

A big fishy (turtle) story

One fall day when we lived in Wisconsin, my father took the family to Coon Forks Dam south of of our farm. I was probably a freshman in high school then. Dad, my younger brother Jim, and I fished while Mom came along for the scenery and fresh air. It looked like there was a nice deep hole just below the dam, and I cast my baited hook into the pool. We fished for some time without any luck, and then my bobber went under. I pulled up to set the hook, but it felt like I had caught the bottom of the river. Nothing moved. I figured I'd hooked onto a submerged tree, and started figuring out how to get unhooked. I walked towards the dam, thinking I might dislodge the hook from a different angle.

Then it began to move! I had something on my hook after all! I reeled in my line very slowly, because this limb, or whatever it was, felt huge.

Eventually it surfaced, and I saw that I had hooked a very large snapping turtle. Dad went down close to the water, and as I the turtle close to shore, he grabbed its tail and hauled it up out of the water.

The critter let out a loud hiss, and my hook came free, fortunately for me. We were trying to decide what to do with it when someone shouted from on top of the dam, "Hey, what are you guys going to do with that turtle?"

A man in his early 30s was waving at us.

"Probably let him go," shouted my father.

"Could I have him?" the guy shouted back.

"If you want him, come and get him!" Dad

responded.

The guy ran to his car, and pretty soon was down beside us with a gunny sack.

"Man, that's a big one!" he exclaimed as he picked up the turtle by his tail and began stuffing him into the sack. "He's bigger than a wash tub!"

"What are you going to do with him?" Dad asked.

"He will make some good turtle soup." came his reply as he carried his heavy bundle to his car.

I don't recall catching any fish that day, but my father often told the turtle story.

"It is not a fish until it's on the bank." Author Unknown

Another of my early fishy stories

One of my rather scary experiences fishing was a trip I took with my parents, my Uncle Bob and Aunt Margaret. I was seven that summer, and we met my parents and them, along with my four-year old cousin Barb to Pike Lake. Our parents rented two row boats, and we went out on the lake. Uncle Bob thought if we fished the deep spots in the lake, we might find some larger fish. We sat for what seemed like hours and at numerous locations with no bites, and no fish. Our mothers had packed lunches, which we ate, throwing bread crusts into the lake to attract some fish. That didn't work, either.

Dad had been watching the skies, because there had been a forecast for rain, but Uncle Bob was certain we would be fine. We rowed to another new location in the middle of the lake. Still no results, and dark clouds were approaching.

Finally, Dad decided that we should head for shore in front of the approaching storm. Uncle Bob agreed and we hoisted the anchors, and the men began rowing towards shore, which was now a long way from where we were.

The storm front reached us before we arrived at the boat dock. Strong winds began to churn the waters, and made rowing difficult. Soon, waves began to lap over the edge of the boats. Barb and I were in tears by now, afraid we would be swept into the lake, and we were driving our parents crazy.

Fortunately, the boats arrived at the dock safely, and we scrambled out onto the ground and shelter from the storm. We didn't catch any fish that day, but were thankful to be on land....

"If people really knew what was important in life, there would be a shortage of fishing rods."

A Pacific Ocean Adventure

During the early 1990's, we traveled west to visit Leslie's parents in Oregon. While we were there, I was invited to go fishing in the Pacific out from Astoria, Washington. Leslie's uncle Duane and our brother-in-law Kevin had made reservations to go out on a charter boat. The three of us men spent the night in an Astoria motel, as the charter boat was scheduled to leave very early the following morning. We ate a light breakfast per Duane's suggestion, as he thought we might get seasick on the boat if we ate greasy food. We left the dock at 6:30, with 12 fishing guests, plus 3 crewmen. We were fishing for King salmon using barb-less hooks, so if we caught fish that were under the size minimum, we could easily shake them off the hook. The crewmen used a paper punch to mark the gill covers of the fish we kept. We were limited to two fish per person, so if anyone caught 3 or more, we could claim our two largest Kings, and the other fish went to other fishermen who hadn't caught a keeper. Our boat limit was 24 fish.

Once we cleared the harbor and got into open water, the boat was greeted with 20 foot waves. The salmon fishing season had opened four days earlier, but this was the first day boats were allowed on open water due to bad weather and high seas. We baited our hooks, and followed directions about trolling. The other fishermen lined up on the port and starboard sides of the boat, while the three of us fished off the stern. Twin diesel inboard motors powered the craft.

The salmon cooperated nicely, and within three hours we had our limit of legal-sized fish, plus one extra that the captain claimed. I had caught three nice fish, plus several smaller ones we had released. The captain had a crewman clean the extra fish, and he began cooking it on a cook stove below, which used diesel fuel.

"I'm contracted for 5 hours on this boat which you guys paid for, so I'm going to cut the engines and we will ride the waves," he announced.

So for the next 1 ½ hours, we watched our boat rise and fall with the waves. Up and down, up and down, up and down! Within 20 minutes or so, every fisherman on that boat was seasick. We, who were fishing off the stern, had also been inhaling the diesel fumes, which may have contributed to us being ill.

After the charter time was up, the captain restarted the engines, and we fought our way through the waves into the harbor and the docks. Once we were in smooth water inside the harbor, the captain asked if anyone wanted a piece of salmon to eat. I was feeling better by then, and ate a few bites, but Kevin and Duane declined.

Once the boat was docked, we divided up our fish. There was a cannery next door, and we could exchange our catch for canned salmon. I took advantage of the offer, as I could easily transport canned salmon back to my Indiana home.

"Nothing makes a fish bigger than almost being caught." Author Unknown

My biggest fish (that I actually did catch)

The next trip we made to Oregon, my brother-in-law Kevin promised to take me fishing in the Columbia River, as the steelhead and coho salmon were coming in from the ocean to spawn upstream. I bought an out-of-state license, borrowed some fishing gear from Kevin, and we headed to the water. He knew of a small, quiet spot along one branch of the river he thought would be productive, and we began fishing.

Soon we both had strikes on our baits, but couldn't catch anything. I moved to another location, and on the fourth cast, had a fish on. I fought him for a time, and finally edged him out of the water onto the sandy beach. What a beautiful fish! He measured 42 inches long, and Kevin was very impressed.

We fished for another hour or so, with no strikes, so we gave up and headed to our in-laws' house. When we arrived, I showed off my fish, then cleaned it. My father-in-law suggested we take it back to Indiana, and called his brother-in-law, Ted, for suggestions on how to ship the fish. Ted took it to one of the hatcheries which had an extremely cold freezer, and suggested that when we left, we should layer it in newspaper inside a suitcase small enough to carry on. We did just that. The salmon was still frozen when we arrived home in Indiana, and it tasted wonderful some weeks later when we baked it.

We ask a simple question
And that is all we wish:
Are fishermen all liars?
Or do only liars fish?
~William Sherwood Fox, *Silken Lines and Silver Hooks*, 1954

Kevin gets a star

During another trip to Oregon, we journeyed to the southern part of the Oregon Pacific Coast. Kevin and I bought tickets on a charter boat, which went out into the ocean about a mile, and anchored so we could fish over the side. Their advertisement suggested we could catch sea bass, grouper, and dozens of other species of fish.

They supplied equipment and all we needed to do was bait the hook and drop it in the water. Sounded like a great deal, and that fish would be rushing to get caught, right? Well....

I managed to catch one fish, the smallest salt water fish I have ever seen, but Kevin did me one better. He caught a starfish! Yeah, that's right, a starfish! I think this belongs in *Ripley's Believe It or Not*. But, like they say, a bad day fishing is still better than a good day at work, and we did have fun and lots of laughs!

"You must be both smart and wise to outwit a fish whose brain is the size of a pea."

Fishing with my grandson

My oldest grandson, Bryan, became my fishing buddy, and when he was old enough to go fishing, I took him to a lake close to where we lived. We found a cove with lily pads and other water plants, which looked to me like a good place to catch pan fish. We readied our tackle, I baited his hook, and cast it out just beyond the weed bed.

"Watch your bobber," I told him, and began to bait my hook.

"Papa," he soon called out, "what should I do?"

His bobber was dancing around on the water as a fish worked on the worm.

"Pull!" I said. "You've got a fish!"

He pulled up on the line, and together we reeled in

a nice perch. Bryan was beside himself with joy.

"I caught my first fish, Papa!" he declared with a huge smile.

"You sure did, Bryan, and that's a nice one." I replied.

I had brought along a bucket, and, after dipping it in the lake for some water, tossed the perch into it.

"Let's see if you can catch another one," I told him as I cast the line out and handed him the fishing rod.

We fished for a good hour and a half longer, with nothing more than a few nibbles, but Bryan had caught his first fish, and he and I were full of joy over his success.

"To fish or not to fish? Now that's a dumb question!"
Author Unknown

Cruise night, a tow truck, and a fishy story

Our city has many old car buffs, and once or twice a year they have a Cruise Night, in which the streets are closed and old collector cars are brought out to cruise down the main drag. They begin at our fairgrounds, and cruise into town past the end of our street. Our grandchildren usually join us at the end of the street to watch the parade of beautiful old vehicles as they cruise by. One evening a few years ago, the kids joined us to watch the cars. Once the paradeof cars passed, Bryan asked if I would take him fishing.

I agreed, and after buying some bait, we headed to one of our area lakes. We had found a nice place next to a boat launch, and we drove over to see if we could catch something with fins.

We got situated with our folding chairs, cast out our bait, and sat quietly, watching the bobbers. We didn't have to wait long, as they were soon dancing on the surface of the waters while fish nibbled on the worms below. Pretty soon Bryan had a nice bluegill on, and expertly reeled it in. We unhooked it, dropped into our waiting bucket, and returned to fishing.

We caught maybe six that evening, including a nice small mouth bass Bryan caught. Boaters floated their motor boats onto and off of their trailers, which they had carefully backed down the boat ramp into the water. All had gone well until we heard some shouting from the ramp. We looked up to see a Jeep and trailer creeping into the water while the owner was attempting to secure his boat to the trailer. He jumped off the trailer, pulled the driver's door open, and hopped into the jeep. By the time he was in, it had backed into the water so far that only part of the top of the vehicle and the hood and windshield were out of the water. The engine was full of water and could not be started.

Here he was, stuck in the lake with no way to get his Jeep, trailer and boat back up the ramp. Several people came to help him, but no one had a chain to pull him out.

"Someone call 911," he pleaded, "my emergency brake gave out!"

Now, a guy with a broken brake had quicky become a very desperate man needing help.

A lady called 911 on her cell phone, explained the situation, and asked for a tow truck. She was told they would have one sent out right away.

Meanwhile, here the young man sat, or rather,

stood, stuck in the water. He had moved out of the Jeep, was standing on the ramp, and had one foot inside his Jeep on the brake. Water was chest high, and if he released the brake, the Jeep would roll deeper into the lake.

We waited a good 10 minutes, and the lady called 911 again, only to be told the tow trucks were all busy, and no one was coming.

When I heard this, I got out my cell phone and called home. I quickly got a phone number of a towing company I knew of. I called, and when Wally answered, the first thing he asked was where I was and if he needed to come and get me.

I explained the situation, and he said, "Give me five minutes. I'm on my way!"

I relayed the message to the waterlogged boater, who thanked me very much. Within the five minutes promised, I saw Wally's tow truck rounding the lake and heading toward us. He backed down the boat ramp, saw what needed to be done, and pulled out a chain. He dove into the water, hooked the chain and his cable to the Jeep, and then started a winch to pull the vehicles out of the water. He had a car carrier, and once he got the Jeep and trailer with boat out of the water and on level ground, he loaded the Jeep and hooked the trailer to his tow bar. Bryan was thoroughly enjoying watching this spectacle take place, as he loved watching heavy equipment in operation.

The Jeep owner said he was an auto mechanic, and directed Wally to his home.

As they drove out of the parking lot, Bryan exclaimed, "Gee, Papa, you saved that man!"

When we got home, he proceeded to tell his parents and everyone else at the house about this adventure, and how I had saved the boater. It felt good receiving the respect of my grandson. Bryan had seen a hundred great old cars, gone fishing, caught fish, and seen a tow truck driver fish a Jeep and trailer out of the lake. All in all, a good day for my fishin' buddy!

"Give a man a fish; he will eat for a day. Teach a man to fish and you will find bait in the fridge." Author Unknown

Bryan's largest fish
(See picture on the front cover.)

A friend of ours from church has a pond on his home property. He stocks it with various fish, and opens it up to friends and special needs individuals to come and fish. He built a small pier out into the water for fishing, making it accessible by those in wheel chairs. He even has a group of blind individuals who come a few times a year to fish.

He had offered use of it to us over the years, and one particular summer day I took my oldest grandson, Bryan, fishing at his pond.

We were fishing from the pier, and Bryan had cast his bait out into the middle of the pond. Ducks were swimming close to us, and I had suggested to Bryan that he not fish near them for fear of catching one on his bait.

Do you see it coming? Yes, he caught a duck! It dove down into the water just after he cast his bait close to it, and the duck took the bait, hook and all! Bryan had quite a fight on his hands for a few moments, until it began taking to the air, and flipped the hook out of its beak.

Once we resumed fishing (for fish), Bryan and I caught some keeper bluegill, and then his bobber went down, headed for the bottom of the lake. I knew the owner had stocked a few bass in his pond, but when Bryan finally got the fish up to the dock, we could see it was a nice catfish, about 14 inches long. He pulled it out of the water, and he was all smiles.

"That's the biggest fish I ever caught!" he exclaimed. "Can we take it home to show Mom?"

I agreed, and we put it in our bucket. Shortly after, I caught a turtle, which we released. After fishing a while longer, we headed home with our catch. I told Bryan he would have to help me clean these fish.

"The rule is, if you catch it, you clean it!"

He had never cleaned fish before, but he agreed. We arrived at the house and proceeded to the back yard to clean fish. We cleaned the bluegill first; I should say, I cleaned the fish, while my grandson watched. But when I got to the catfish, and cutting it produced blood, Bryan disappeared. I turned around and saw that he was now watching from our deck, one floor above the back yard. Now Bryan advocates "catch and release" so he doesn't have to witness cleaning fish, or worse yet, clean them himself.

A fisherman's prayer
"Thank you, Lord, for the life you have given me, and forgive me when I take it for granted. Thank you for the sunshine and the rain. Thank you for the opportunity to get up in the morning to go fishing. And, thank you in advance, as I won't be as thankful at 3:00 a.m. Amen."

A chance for some lunkers on Lake Michigan

A few years ago we had the opportunity to go on a charter boat fishing for salmon and lake trout on the big lake we live near, Lake Michigan. An acquaintance of ours ran a charter boat on weekends in the fall and spring, and during the summer when he wasn't working at school. I contacted a friend from church, who was also interested.

We met at the dock in Michigan City, where our friend Jeff kept his boat. The skies were clear, and the lake, while not totally calm, had some very mild rolls.

"Beautiful day to go fishing!" exclaimed Jeff.

I introduced Denny, my church friend, who had brought along one of his sons and a grandson, and my grandson Bryan, and his uncle (my son) Tony. Jeff provided lunch and water along with all the tackle we needed for the charter. His father was along to operate the boat, and Jeff instructed us on how to catch our finny friends. The eight of us cruised out of the harbor and into open lake water.

Jeff got all the down riggers situated, lures ready,

and gave the signal for us to drop them into the water. His dad was monitoring a fish finder he had onboard, and began seeing images of fish below us. He would then try to maneuver the boat so our lures passed over or near the fish.

Soon we had a strike. We had to reel in our spinners so the one with the fish wouldn't get tangled up with the other lines.

Once the fish was near the boat, Jeff drooped a net over the stern of the boat, and we had our first fish, a nice coho salmon, about 24" long. Lures went back into the water, and we were set for the next fish.

My plan was to catch a salmon, and then let Bryan or Tony pull one in. At least, that was my plan. They had moved back into the cabin portion of the boat. Both of them were now looking rather pale.

"If you want to catch a fish, you have to come out and take a turn with a rod."

Tony looked up at me. "My stomach isn't feeling very good, Dad."

Bryan also nodded his head, and I could see the motion of the boat was getting to him, too.

"Okay. Let me see if I can find something to help."

I found some lemon-lime soda in the drink cooler, and gave each of them one.

I hoped the soda might help settle their stomachs, and take their minds off the rolling motion of the boat. I went back out to wait my turn to catch a fish.

Soon I hooked one about the same size as the one we had taken previously. Under Jeff's excited instructions, I brought it in. Soon we had a third one on.

I went back to check on my guys. Tony was using the head (nautical talk for a bathroom), and Bryan looked miserable.

Seeing there was nothing I could do, I returned to the stern of the boat, where Denny was busy with a fish.

"He's got a dandy," said Jeff. "See how the rod is bent? I hope he can get it in without losing it. I'd like to find some more like this one."

Denny successfully landed his fish, which proved to be our biggest catch of the day.

The guys felt much better after we got our feet on dry land again. I believe we ended up with a total of eight salmon that day, with Denny's being the largest.

But I'm not sure if I can get Tony and Bryan back on a charter boat again.

"Some people fish best with a lit cigar. Others use bait."

A fishing day at the park

Two summers ago, Leslie and I packed up three of our grandkids and went to a city park close to their home. There is a nice pond in the park with a creek running through it. A fountain in the middle is used to aerate the water, and it's stocked occasionally with fish by the park service.

We found a nice place along the water's edge, I put down my folding chair to claim my territory, and began baiting hooks. Layla, our youngest granddaughter, was first. I helped her cast out her bait, showed her how the rod and spinning reel worked, and turned to my next tackle setup for our youngest grandson, Jackson. I no sooner got his hook baited than Layla began yelling.

"Papa, I got something!"

Indeed she had; a small bluegill had obligingly taken her worm and gotten hooked in the process. Layla reeled in the fish with my instruction, and promptly swung it my direction, smacking me in the face with it.

"Can you take it off the hook, Papa?"

I got Jackson's worm into the water, and then started working on Layla's fish. It was small, so I let it slip back into the pond. Meanwhile, Bryan, our oldest grandson, had baited his hook and cast it out into deeper water. He soon had a fish of his own.

I fixed Layla's hook and worm, cast it out in the water for her, and, as I was turning around, Jackson was yelling, "I got one! I got one!"

He was able to bring it in with help. Another bluegill, this time big enough to keep. I took it off the hook, and asked, "Are we keeping them?"

I got a yes from Jackson, no from Bryan, and now it was Layla who had the winning vote.

"No, Papa, I think we should let it go."

The votes were cast, the decision made. The bluegill went back to join his comrades and be caught another day.

The grandchildren kept me busy that afternoon baiting hooks and unhooking fish. Jackson touched worms and became my worm man, handing one to me when I needed to bait a hook. Layla wanted to release the second fish that she caught herself, so I showed her how to handle it, and she released it and several more. Bryan was doing great at casting his bait, and Layla and Jackson were also doing an acceptable job by the time the day was done.

Bryan pointed out a blue heron in the shadows along the other side of the pond, and we watched him hunt for his meal. It was very interesting to watch him stand motionless for a long time, watching for fish, water bugs, frogs, and whatever else he could find. He didn't seem to mind our presence, as long as we kept our distance.

By the time we were ready to leave, Layla had caught the first fish, and a total of twelve, including a small bass that jumped several times for her. This fish was also the largest catch. Jackson was one behind her, with eleven, including a very small bluegill, giving him honors for the smallest fish. Bryan didn't fare quite as well as his brother and sister, but thoroughly enjoyed catching and releasing the fish. It was a wonderful day in the park, with grandma Leslie cheering on the fishing kids.

"I spent most of my money on fishing. The rest I wasted." Author Unknown

In Pursuit of the Mighty Muskie

An acquaintance of mine, who heard I was writing a book of fishing stories, submitted the following tale to be included. He asked for $50 and a copy of the finished book in exchange. It remains to be seen if I made the right choice, but I am pleased (I guess) to introduce you to Marvin Smith's fishing story.

A year ago this past spring, I had paid a visit to my doctor for my annual checkup. The doctor gave me a good report, but felt I needed more exercise, now that I was in my mid-forties. He asked what I was doing for recreation and physical activity.

"I don't really have any hobbies or sports activities which take me outside," I replied. "I do some exercising indoors, but it is limited."

"I suggest you look into some outdoor sport activity to get some real exercise and fresh air. Do you golf? Swim? What about jogging or hiking? I might even suggest biking or kayaking."

I thought about these suggestions for a few moments.

"What about fishing?" I asked.

"That at least will get you outdoors, and if you do some rowing or canoeing, that would be good exercise. Are you a fisherman?"

"I'm willing to learn."

"Very well, then. I would like to see you in three

months to see how you've progressed."

I stopped at the county library and picked up several books about fishing, including "How to Fish For Dummies," and spent the next several days studying about the art of fishing. That Saturday, I went to a sport shop and selected a tackle box, a fishing hat, shirt, pants and vest, along with some nice boat shoes. The salesman saw me looking at rods and reels, and asked what type of fishing I would be doing.

"I've been reading up on types of fish I'd like to catch, and I decided to try muskellunge. What do I need to catch them?"

The salesman began rubbing his hands. "You need some hefty gear for Muskie," he said with a smile. "You've come to just the right place!"

Reaching up on a rack, he brought down a fishing rod that looked like a small pine tree without limbs.

"This is what I recommend; this is a Muskie Whacker, made by Schmidt, and here is a reel to go with it."

He picked up a huge reel that looked like a small winch with a huge crank. "You put 35 pound test line on this, and you will be set. Where do you fish?"

"I'm headed to Hayward, Wisconsin, the Muskie capital!"

"That's a good place to start. Now, what are you going to land this fish with?"

He sold me a huge net with an extension handle, a beautiful set of waders, a tape measure to check the fish's length, and a scale to weigh it after I catch it. He then handed me a knife.

"This is a must for fishing! It is very sharp, light weight, easy to carry, and something you will definitely need on your trip."

I opened the knife and looked at the glistening blade.

"Did I tell you it's very sharp?" he asked, then motioned to my hand.

I had closed the knife, and in the process I cut myself, and blood was running down my hand and dripping on the floor of the store.

"I'm not very good with knives," I said as I retrieved my hanky from my pocket and began wiping the blood from my hand.

"You will need one of these, too," the salesman said as he handed me a large first-aid kit. "I also recommend a pair of Polarized sun glasses, so you can see fish in the water.

"Now, what are you going to fish with? Lures or live bait?'

"What do you recommend?"

"You should be prepared for both, depending upon what lake you go to, and what the weather conditions are. I'd suggest you take hooks for bait fishing and I have some artificial bait I can recommend."

He steered me to hooks large enough to tow my lawn tractor with, some heavy duty stainless steel leaders (Muskies have very sharp teeth, you know), a couple of bobbers the size of my fist, and then he took me to the artificial lures.

"I recommend this one to start," he said, handing me a bright red fish-shaped jointed plug as big as my foot. It had five sets of treble hooks hanging from its sides and rear. It looked nasty.

"This is called the Muskie Honey. Guaranteed to drive a fish nuts. It'll catch anything!"

"How do I fish with this?"

"Use this for casting or trolling, if trolling is allowed on the lake. Lots of smaller lakes don't allow trolling anymore. Oh, and here are a couple more plugs and some spinners."

He handed me two more fish-shaped lures, as big as the first one, a bait called a "spoon" which was larger than my shoehorn, and several spinners with bright, shiny feathers and huge hooks in the business end. I looked at the tackle box I was holding, and realized I needed to go bigger.

"You will need a deluxe tackle box. It will accommodate large plugs and spinners."

I grabbed one, then prepared to check out. I thought the register was going to overheat by the time he got everything wrung up and presented me with the total. The red lure alone cost $35!

I handed him my credit card, finished the transaction, and headed to my car, thinking how fortunate I was to find such a knowledgeable salesman to take care of me! Besides, I looked at this not as a big expense, but an investment in my health and my future.

As my wound from the knife was still bleeding, I decided to swing by the doctor's office to have it checked.

Two hours later, I left with three stitches in my finger, and instructions from the doctor to stay away from knives.

I spent the next several hours planning my vacation trip to Wisconsin in pursuit of the mighty Muskie. I found on the internet a great place to stay just a few miles from the city of Hayward at Lake Flapjack Resort. I had vacation time coming from work, fishing season was open, and I made reservations for the following night. Beware, Muskies, here I come!

The trip north took me nearly ten hours, including stops, and I arrived at the resort around 7:30 that evening. The resort was a few years older than the pictures on the internet, but the lake was gorgeous. I checked in and the lady at the desk directed me to my cabin.

I unloaded and prepared for a my day tomorrow.

I went to bed early. Plans were to be up at 6:00, grab a quick breakfast at the resort tavern, and go after Muskies.

Something woke me up a half hour later. Something was scratching on the floor. I turned on a light, and saw a small critter run under the dresser. Mice! I thought, but saw another head out of the bathroom. They were chipmunks! What were they doing in my cabin?

I got out of bed, chased the two furry invaders out of the bedroom, and called to the main desk.

"There are chipmunks in my cabin!" I complained into the phone.

"And?" came the response.

"I don't want chipmunks in my cabin!"

"They don't eat much, and they won't crawl onto

the bed. Usually."

"I didn't pay for chipmunks in my cabin, and I don't want them here!"

"Sorry, but they get into all the cabins."

"Where can I rent a room without chipmunks?"

"The nearest resort in 50 miles from here, and they don't have any rooms available. I already checked for another customer."

"What am I supposed to do?"

"Get a good night's sleep, I reckon," said the night clerk as she hung up.

Morning came about 5:30 as I woke up, opened the pickup truck door, and crawled out to get the kinks out of my joints. I cautiously entered the cabin to find the chipmunks had vacated the premises sometime in the night. I showered, put my fishing duds on, and headed into the tavern for breakfast. Odors of bacon, sausage and beer met me at the door.

"What'll it be?" asked a heavy set lady in her sixties.

"Bacon, two eggs over easy, and hash browns"

"How about three flapjacks with blueberries?"

"What's wrong with bacon and eggs?"

"Ran out 20 minutes ago."

"Who ordered them?"

"Had sixteen guys in here from Iowa. Cleaned me out."

"Where are they now? I don't see anyone but me."

"They be out on the lake already, fishin' fer Muskies. Gotta get up early fer Muskies."

I settled for flapjacks, over-cooked and thin, with blueberry syrup (she was out of blueberries and maple syrup), coffee thicker than paint, and a glass of water with particles of rust in the bottom. I paid a very high price for breakfast, and headed out to the pier, where I hoped to rent a boat.

I introduced myself to an elderly man sitting in a rickety rocking chair in front of an old boathouse, which had seen better days.

"Sam Smiling Fox, at your service."

"Mr. Fox, I want to rent a boat."

"Nope. No boats available. They're all out on the lake. By the way, it's Mr. Smiling Fox, not Mr. Fox."

"Any boats available later today?'

"Can't say. I rent by the day, not the hour."

I turned to leave, then turned back.

"I'm curious about your name. Are you from a local Wisconsin tribe?"

"Nope. Came from the southwest. Arizona, in particular. I'm from the Flat Black tribe."

"I've never heard of the Flat Blacks."

"They were originally from the Flathead tribe and the Black Feet Nation, both from Montana. They intermarried, and neither tribe would claim them, so they became nomads until they found some desert land in Arizona, which they laid claim to. I'm fourth generation Flat Black."

"How did you end up in northern Wisconsin?"

"Hated desert. Loved lakes. Settled here. Been here over forty years."

"Thank you, Mr. Smiling Fox. Is it alright if I fish from the pier, seeing as there are no boats available?"

"Got a license? Tavern sells them. Out of state, I presume?"

"I'm from Indiana. First time fishing."

He looked me over from head to toe and nodded his head. "Thought so! Creeps and idiots cannot hide for long on a fishing trip."

"Is that an old Indian proverb?"

"Yep!"

I went into the tavern, paid for my out-of-state license, and returned to the pier. I had my rod and reel set to go, took out my red lure, attached it to my stainless steel leader, and made my first ever cast. I felt an extreme pain in my backside. My lure, which was guaranteed to catch anything, had caught me! It had ripped a hole in the butt of my fishing pants, and was now stuck in my flesh. I reached around and dislodged the hook, but stuck my finger with one of the sharp points of the lure. Catching my breath, I tried a second cast. My red lure went sailing out into the lake. A beautiful cast, but something was stuck to my bait this time. I soon recognized it as my new fishing hat. I began to reel in, only to see that my reel looked like a bird's nest, with line wound around everything; loops here and there; a total mess. I sat down on the dock and began to untangle the reel.

I fought with it for ten minutes before I got the tangles cleared out, and I could reel in my lure and fishing hat. My red lure had long since sunk to the bottom of the lake. Once I got the line tight, I made about four turns of the handle and the lure stopped. It was hung up on something.

I moved around the pier, my rod arcing, as I attempted to dislodge the stubborn lure. Finally I got it loose, and guided the lure in, sans hat. I had lost my fishing hat to some log laying at the bottom of the lake!

I composed myself, reset the drag on my reel, and prepared to cast out my bait once again, hopefully without any articles of clothing or skin attached to the hooks. The lure sailed up, up, up into the air, where a gust of wind caught it and blew it into the upper branch of a tree limb over the water. The lure wrapped itself at least three times around the limb before it stopped, and hung there, swinging back and forth.

Taking a deep sigh, I looked around to see if I could retrieve the lure without falling into the lake or falling out of the tree. Seeing no other options, I took out my trusty fishing knife, cut the line, and faced the facts that after just losing a lure that had cost me $35, I would have to try something different.

I took a new stainless steel leader from my tackle box, tied it to my line, and took out one of my spinners.

"Let's see what this baby will do."

I cast it out into the lake without difficulties this time, and began reeling it in. Something hit it. Hard! I pulled up on the rod, and I had a fight on my hands. I fought the fish for a good 15 minutes, pulled it up to the dock, and, using my net, pulled it out of the water. I had caught a long silvery fish, a real beauty. My first ever Muskie! I pulled out my tape to measure my trophy.

I looked at the tape in shock; 36 inches.

Wisconsin's minimum length for a legal fish was 40 inches. My catch was 4 inches too short! I took a selfie photo using my phone while holding up the fish, then sadly returned it to the lake. Well, I had caught a Muskie, but it was too small.

I walked to the end of the pier, and cast my spinner out into the lake again, keeping it away from tree branches, weeds and logs. But in my excitement, my fishing rod slipped out of my hand and went soaring into the water.

Oh, no! What have I done? As I looked down into the clear lake water, I could see my rod and reel laying at the bottom. An idea hit me. I had bought waders, right? Well, dummy, put them on, wade out, and retrieve your equipment. I went to my pickup and put on my waders.

I eased off the middle section of the pier, where it sagged into the water. Good, I was only in water just above my knees. I gently made my way to the end of the pier. Good! The water was only waist high. My rod lay some ten yards ahead of me. I let go of the pier and eased out deeper. Only five yards to go. Three yards, two yards, I'm there! Now, all I need to do is reach down....

I didn't realize it as I bent into the water to grab the rod, but I had a new problem! As I grabbed the fishing rod, water rushed over the top of my waders and quickly filled them. The shock of the cold water flood stunned me for a moment. I stood up, with rod in hand, and fell backwards into the lake.

When I tried to stand up, I couldn't get back on my feet, and my waders, now filled with water, were pulling me down. Not being a good swimmer, I was struggling to keep my head above water, and not succeeding.

Out of nowhere, a hand reached down and grabbed my shirt, pulling me up to the surface. Once I straightened up, I kept my head above water. Sam Smiling Fox had rescued me.

He helped me of the water, and I struggled out of my waders.

"Thank you so much, Mr. Smiling Fox. I could have drowned! I owe you my life."

He just nodded in agreement. "Dumb Hoosier!" he said as he headed back to the boathouse. "There is a fine line between fishing and falling off the dock like an idiot."

"Is that another old Indiana proverb?"

"Yep"

Fortunately, I had held on to my fishing rod. I gathered my tackle and my waders and headed toward my cabin to change clothes.

After I cleaned up and took a much-needed rest, I found a family restaurant just five miles from the cabin. I bought a good meal of chicken noodle soup, a burger and fries, and a GOOD cup of coffee. I really had needed this after my first fishing day.

The next morning I was up before dawn, stretched the kinks out of my legs and back, and left the truck to enter the cabin, chase out the chipmunk invaders, and prepare for the day. I bought a doughnut (at least a week old) at the tavern and ate it with water for breakfast. Then, I headed to the boathouse.

"Sorry, no motorboats. The only thing I got today is a rowboat. All the motorboats is rented again."

I paid $35 for a day rental of a row boat, put my rod, tackle, net, and everything else I needed into the boat and prepared to head out.

"Where can I find some Muskie?" I asked.

"In the lake," Sam Smiling Fox said.

"Where in the lake?"

"Well, you might head up around that dogleg right," he replied, pointing out across the lake.

"I caught one off the pier yesterday, but it was too small, so I threw it back in."

"Ain't no Muskie here," he said flatly. "They don't hang around this pier."

"By some miracle, my phone survived the lake dousing. I took a picture of it."

I showed him the picture I had taken.

"He ain't got no spots! That there is a pike! It's a big one, too. You threw it back?'

Feeling even more foolish than I had yesterday, I nodded my head.

"Dumb Hoosier!" he said under his breath."If you teach a man to fish, you feed him for a lifetime. But if you just give him a pole, he'll have to teach himself."

"Is that another wise old Indian proverb?"

"Yep!"

"Who is the wise Indian you keep quoting?"

"Me! I'm the wise old Indian. Now, to your question. There's a dogleg right that leads to a cove with lots of weeds. You might find a Muskie there. But you'll want to stay out of the weeds. Weeds and fishin' don't mix."

"A dogleg? I thought Lake Flapjack was named for its shape."

"Not hardly, it was named after the first settler who built a cabin here, Willard 'Flapjack' Washington. Did you know he invented the flapjack?"

"I think the pancake dates back to the early Greeks. They brought the idea to America centuries ago."

"Don't know anything about Greeks, only what Flapjack Washington told me before he died. There's a plaque over there what tells it all."

He motioned to the small parking lot where I saw a weathered piece of barn wood leaning against the fence.

"What do you think I should use for Muskie today?" I asked.

He looked into my tackle box, and shook his head.

"Dumb Hoosier," he muttered, then louder, stated, "You can lead a horse to drink, but you can't make him water!"

"What was that? Is that another old Indian proverb?"

"Yep. But to answer your question, you'd be best off using live bait today. I got sucker minnows for sale."

I bought half a dozen, and put them in my minnow bucket along with my tackle. I hopped into the boat, and rowed toward the dogleg in the lake.

"Doc. Ketchem would be pleased with me today," I told my minnow bucket as I worked the boat into the cove. "I'm certainly getting my exercise."

I came into the beautiful small cove full of confidence. A weed bed extended from the shore about four feet, with a few lily pads on the outer edge. The lake was clear of obstructions after that; no tree limbs, no snags or stumps. It was a gorgeous sunny day for fishing.

I anchored on the edge of the weed bed, and prepared to fish. I put a huge hook on the leader, hooked it through a sucker like I had read about, clipped my large bobber about three feet up, and tossed it over the side of the boat, making certain to hang onto the rod. I was Muskie fishing! I couldn't wait for my first bite.

I sat there, watching the bobber waltz around the lake as the sucker swam around under water. I watched the sun rise in the sky, becoming hot as the day progressed. I moved my bait periodically when it got too close to my boat. I examined my finger, where the stitches were; it had gotten infected and was sore to the touch. I watched some mallards taking their newly hatched ducklings out for the day. A deer fly landed on my knee, and I swatted it, flicking it into the water. I watched as water came into the boat.

I realized I had a problem; I was taking on water, and getting my new boat shoes wet! But, from where?

I looked around the boat and found a drain plug in the stern that was leaking. The drain plug was loose. I messed with it, getting it to tighten, but by now I had some two inches of water in the boat. I thought about rowing back to the dock, but figured a little water wouldn't hurt me, as long as I had stopped the leak. Besides, I wanted to catch a Muskie.

I made myself comfortable with my feet out of the water, and must have dozed off. When I came to my senses, I noticed my bobber had moved deeply into the weed bed. I began to reel in my bait. Unfortunately, the sucker had successfully wound my fishing line around some weeds.

I began to tug on my rod in an attempt to dislodge the bait. No luck. It was hung up on some very stubborn weeds.

Irritated, I began to pull hard with my fishing rod. If I used enough force, maybe I could rip the weeds out of the water. My force on the rod began to pull my boat into the weeds. I thought this would help; maybe I could pull myself close to my hook and pull it loose.

I couldn't get close enough, so with one mighty tug on the rod, I ripped everything out of the water. The hook, my black sucker, and a huge weed, roots and all, came flying up into the air, and landed whap! onto the back of my neck. The weight of the weeds and bait impaled the hook in my neck! The weeds and sucker came loose and slithered down inside my shirt. But that hook went deep into my flesh! I yelled, dropped the fishing rod, and reached up to extract the hook. It was stuck, and it really hurt!

Furthermore, as I was now deep into weeds and close to shore, mosquitoes had found me. A huge swarm flew around me, looking for warm flesh to suck blood.

Realizing I needed help, I got out my fish knife, cut the line to the hook (and another finger) as I worked on the line, pulled up the anchor, and began rowing for dear life back to the dock. Sam Smiling Fox could help remove the hook, I was certain.

I rowed away from the cloud of bloodsucking

mosquitoes, around the dogleg, and soon had the dock in sight. As I pulled up, Sam was sitting in front of the boathouse in his rocking chair.

"I need your help!" I called, sweat rolling down my face, and blood running down my back. "I got a fishhook stuck in my neck, and can't get it out!"

He helped me out of the rowboat and took a look at my bleeding neck.

"Wow. You got that thing in there deep. The barb won't let it loose, either," he exclaimed as he moved the hook around, trying to extract it and wiping blood with an old towel. "You need a doctor to get this out. I **could** cut it out, I guess."

I looked up and saw a large rusty knife he had pulled out of a scabbard.

"How close is the nearest doctor?" I asked, wisely.

"There's an emergency medical care office about 10 miles north," he said, putting his knife away.

He went into the boathouse and came back with a business card.

"I keep these handy in case of accidents," he said. "We get many inexperienced fishermen here. Had a guy nearly cut his finger off a day ago. Some guy from Iowa."

I thanked him, and I heard him mutter "dumb Hoosier" as I got in my truck.

"The doctor will see you now." said an elderly nurse/receptionist, as she ushered me into a small room. "Doctor Tater will be in soon."

Doctor Tater was a young man, appearing like he was barely out of high school. He looked at my neck and shook his head.

"How did you manage this? I've never seen anyone hook themselves this badly."

I told him the story as he readied a huge syringe.

"This will sting for a moment, then go numb. Once it does, I can cut out the hook. Probably a couple of stitches, but it will be fine in a week or two. What are you going to do about the sunburn?"

"Sunburn? What sunburn?"

He motioned me to a mirror, where a bright red face glared back at me with two white rings around the eyes where my sunglasses had been. I realized my face and arms were starting to burn.

"When did you last have a tetanus shot?"

"I have no idea. Years ago, I'd guess."

He left the room and returned with two more syringes.

"Which arm should I use?" he asked.

"Left one, I guess."

Doctor Tater explained the second shot would help with the sunburn, and told me to expect my skin to blister before it peels. He administered the shots, and handed me a large tube of ointment.

"This is severe burn ointment. It will help with pain. Use it as much and as frequently as you need, and you **will** need it. Your family doctor can prescribe more for you. Now, let's look at those cuts on your fingers."

He put two stitches in my fresh cut, drained infection out of my previous cut, and bandaged both fingers. Two hours later, I left the doctor's office with three stitches, a numb neck, more stitches in my fingers, the tube of ointment, and red skin burning like fire.

I drove back to the cabin, loaded my clothes and gear into my pickup, and went to my cabin to lay down. I chased chipmunks out of the room, slathered more ointment on my face, neck, ears, arms and hands, and laid down. I was in pain, and needed some rest.

I slept for about an hour, and awoke to hear a chipmunk party going on in the cabin. They were chasing each other everywhere, including across the bed. My mosquito bites were itching, and I couldn't scratch them because of my burning skin. I'd had enough!

I got up, chased the creepy critters out of the room, packed my belongings, and painfully and slowly made my way to my pickup. The resort clerk was working outside, so I handed her my key.

"I'm headed home."

I noticed a group of fisherman at the dock, all carrying some huge fish.

"What did those guys catch?"

"Why, that's the group from Iowa, and they caught a number of Muskies."

"What were they using for bait?"

"Chipmunks."

I rolled up my window, turned on the air conditioning, and headed south. I made several stops on the way home to put ointment on my sunburn, and was very relieved upon my arrival home.

When I walked into the bedroom some time after 4:00 a.m., my wife hardly recognized me. She thought I was an intruder coming into the bedroom to murder her. Fortunately, she recognized my voice when I called her by name, and she put her pistol back into the night stand drawer.

A week later, I went to my doctor to have the stitches removed. After relating my fishing adventure, I told him I was retiring from Muskie fishing, as it was too hazardous for my health. He agreed.

"What activity do you think you might try next? You still need exercise and fresh air."

"I've been reading some magazines on hunting. I think I might go turkey hunting."

"What do you know about guns?"

"I've been reading up, and I know a great sports shop."

As I was leaving Doc Ketchem's office, I noticed him just shaking his head.

"Dumb Hoosier," he muttered.

A final note; A couple days after Smith left on a Georgia hunting trip, I got the following message from him.

"I'm in a hospital here in Georgia; seems I shot myself in the foot while hunting some wild boar, but I'm expected to be back to normal in a couple weeks. Only shot off a little toe, and it's healing. I should be heading home as soon as I can travel and they finish the body work on my pickup.

"Say, what do you know about skiing?"

I have not answered him as yet.

As a followup to this Muskie story, I contacted the Lake Flapjack Resort and talked at length with Sam Smiling Fox. He verified this tale, but I was concerned about his story of the Flat Black Native American Tribe. This is what he told me.

"The Flat Black tribe did exist for some 80 or so years, and were finally taken in by the Blackfoot Nation some 15 years ago. The Flat Blacks did leave their mark in history.

"They had a small uprising between their small tribe and a neighboring tribe, the Navahochies. They went to war, but ran out of arrows during their first battle. Both tribes settled on a truce, smoked a peace pipe, and went back home to their squaws.

"The Flat Blacks were the originators of the porta-potty. They realized they needed privacy, and, as there were few if any trees of size where they camped, they dug a pit, put a bench with holes over it, and erected a small teepee over everything. They called it their "Peetee" and it was very popular with their tribal members.

"They also claim to have invented toilet paper. The few trees where they camped had very small leaves. So, they rendered the juices from the cacti in the area to make fire water, and saved the fibers from the cacti, dried them, and produced a paper-like substance. They just had to make certain they removed all the needles."

Time for a fishing joke.

Two parrots were sitting on a perch. The one said to the other, "Do you smell something fishy?"

Another limerick

I had a friend who owned a runabout,
and kept it in Lake Sauerkraut.
He fished on a weekend
with his brand new girlfriend,
and hit her in the face with a trout.
(She's no longer his girlfriend, no doubt!)

"Wanted: Good woman – Must be able to clean, cook, sew, dig worms and clean fish. Must have boat and motor. Please send picture of boat and motor." Author Unknown

Poetry Time

Some of us more experienced individuals may remember this old nursery rhyme from our childhood.

Fishy fishy in a brook
Papa catch 'em with a hook
Mama fry 'em in a pan
Baby eat 'em like a man

Here is my poem based upon this rhyme.

Little fishy in the brook
Come and bite my shiny hook

I baited it an hour ago;
Why must you be so darned slow?
I was here at the crack of dawn,
scared away a doe and fawn.
Settled by this pretty brook,
stuck my finger with my hook
trying to get the worm on right
so you fishies will take a bite.
But you disappoint me, as time passes.
Won't you nibble, big black basses?
My bobber wobbles to and fro
as the summer breezes blow
but nary a nibble do I get;
you haven't moved my bobber yet!
"Ribbit, ribbit" sings a frog
sitting on a hollow log.
Guess he sings his lovelorn song
to his loved one all day long.
Ho, at last I got a bite
and too soon I make my strike
to find my hook the worm is taken
and my strategy of fishing, beaten.
My hopes of catching mister trout
is dashed it seems, there is no doubt.
Perhaps it best my tackle I take
over to that yonder lake
and see what finny fish I find
while I'm in that frame of mind
that I can conquer the simple fish
and true will come my morning wish.
Big, big fishy in the lake,

won't you find my bait to take?
I will catch you if I can,
and show you to my frying pan.
Open some chips and a cold drink.
By George, I'm getting hungry, I think.

Time now for another good fishing joke

Two older men were sitting at a lake fishing, where they met nearly every Thursday during fishing season. They had become friends, but never talked much about their families. They observed some flashing lights approaching them. A funeral procession came slowly down the street and headed across a bridge near them. Charlie stood up, and, removing his hat, watched solemnly as the hearse passed by.

"Charlie, that was nice of you to pay respect to the deceased." said Norm.

"It was the least I could do. I was married to her for forty two years."

Camping our way west

"We are going west to Oregon, and we are going to pull some pop-up campers. We will camp on the way, and be in Oregon in five or six days. Doesn't that sound like fun?"

This is the message I got from my wife, Leslie, when I got home from work. I had two weeks' vacation scheduled in a few days, and we had planned to go west.

But, camping never came up in the conversation, until now.

"My parents (Pete and Shirley) have a camper, Uncle Carl and Aunt Florence have a camper, and my brother Michael and cousin Becky are going with us," Leslie stated. "We leave Friday as soon as we get home from work. I've started packing, and I think it will be loads of fun. Think of the things we will see, and camp grounds are much less expensive than motel rooms."

"OK by me, I guess. The campers will each sleep four?"

"As many as six, if needed. My parents have it all worked out with Carl and Florence. We travel from NW Indiana into Iowa the first night. We should be settled by nine, and we are taking along sandwiches to eat for dinner, so we won't have to stop anywhere."

Friday afternoon came, and everyone was at our house when we arrived home.

"All set?" my mother-in-law, Shirley, asked. "You ride up front with Pete. Leslie and I will ride in the back and talk."

I sneezed, got into the car, and we headed west into the sun.

"What's wrong, Honey?" asked Leslie, after I sneezed several more times.

"This started at work today. I just started sneezing, and have a runny nose. I'll be OK."

This, however, was not the case, as a cold was apparently coming onto me quickly. Sneezes and sniffles kept me busy as we traveled.

We crossed the Illinois state line into Iowa, and

began looking for a campground. Aunt Florence had brought a campground guide, and it was up to me, as navigator, to find a suitable campground. I located one just a few miles into the state, we decided it sounded fine, and we headed there to camp. They had space available, we payed and pulled into two vacant spots, and popped the campers up. We were all tired, and in bed by about 9:30.

A loud crash of thunder woke us all by 11:00. We were under a severe thunderstorm warning, with high winds. Moments later, the rain began, and became a downpour.

We tried to sleep, but soon the winds picked up. It was strong enough to move the pull-outs we were sleeping on. We began to fear our campers would blow over.

Seeing no letup in the storm, we decided to fold in the campers, drop them down, and drive west to see if we could get out of the storm.

I was really feeling ill by then, so Leslie and Pete jumped out into the driving rain to collapse the camper. They were drenched by the time they got back into the car, and Leslie had injured her hand in the camper. We pulled out of the campground and headed west.

We drove for several hours in the rain,

By the time we arrived in Amana, Iowa, we were out of the rain. We ate breakfast, and the ladies wanted to visit a museum and some gift shops, so we men found a city park and opened up the campers to dry out the canvas.

Our next night we spent in the vast, flat state of

Nebraska. We selected a campground which featured a swimming pool, as some of us thought a dip before bedtime would be fantastic.

We paid our money, popped up the campers, and looked for the pool, only to find out that it was a horse trough! The grounds had an outhouse for guests to use. And, for added entertainment, we heard melodious voices of coyotes or wolves singing their forlorn songs of lost loves. Becky was so afraid of them that Michael had to stand guard outside the outhouse to protect her from any marauders.

We were rolling early the next morning, and passed through Jackson Hole, Wyoming, camping at the base of the grand Tetons. It had been a beautiful, cloudless day to travel, and we crawled into sleeping bags early that night. As the sun went down, though, so did the temperature. We had to get up and put coats on to keep warm that night in our sleeping bags.

We woke up early the next morning to find Carl and Florence up with a campfire going. Florence was trying to make coffee, but the water in the coffee pot she had filled the night before had frozen. We certainly did not expect temperatures to be this cold in August. But, when the sun started hitting the mountain tops, it was an absolutely gorgeous sight that morning; one that will stay with me the rest of my life.

Our next leg of the trip was uneventful until evening. We stopped in Western Idaho that night, and Carl discovered a problem when he began to crank up the camper. The cable had snapped, and he couldn't get the camper open. They still had access to the lower part of it, so they could get clothes out. They decided they would crawl through the door and sleep on the camper floor that night. We had room in our camper for the others, Michael and Becky.

We found Carl and Florence sleeping in their car the next morning.

"We couldn't sleep in that camper," Florence said. "It felt like a coffin!"

We arrived at our destination that next day at the home of Shirley's and Florence's sister, Lois, in Boring, Oregon, which would be our home base.

So, what does this have to do with fishing? I'm getting to that.

One of the things I wanted to do while I was in Oregon was to go fishing. We had little fishing equipment at Aunt Lois's house, so she suggested we go up to a trout farm close to them.

A trout farm is a series of ponds where fish are raised. You go there to fish, no license is required, and they charge you by the inch for the fish you catch and keep. This sounded like a good idea to me.

We arrived at the trout farm, and they had different pools with different sized fish in each pond. They explained that they bought small rainbow trout from the hatcheries and kept them in the ponds as they grew. Once they reached over 24 inches, they had to release them to the wilds, as they were now considered steelhead. We used barb-less hooks, and canned corn for bait. I caught three fish from the pond which held the biggest fish. They cleaned the fish for us, and we were down the road after paying for them. We had a wonderful fish dinner that evening.

"Let's go hiking today, what d'ya say?" asked Shirley the next day. "There is a trail that goes down Larch Mountain to Multnomah Falls, and the weather is perfect today for a walk."

The consensus was in favor of this trek, so we all piled into two cars and drove the short distance to the mountain top. We found the trail, which had a marker announcing "Multnomah Falls 9 Mi." Shirley volunteered that she and Pete would drive the cars down to the trail's end. The hikers were Leslie and I, Carl and Florence, Aunt Lois and Ted, Michael, Becky, and Leslie's Uncle Duane. We were wearing everyday clothes and shoes, not hiking gear or shoes. Nine miles should be just an easy walk, right? We weren't carrying food or water; just an afternoon walk.

"We'll see you at the bottom in a couple hours," Shirley said as they drove off.

We began our journey. The path was smooth, wide, and easy to follow. We walked for some time, and felt we were doing well. We met a few hikers coming from the other direction, and I noticed many had on hiking gear and were using walking sticks or poles, but I thought nothing of it.

After an hour and a half, we stopped to rest for a few minutes. Lois and Ted were both in their sixties at the time, so we were concerned about them. They seemed to be doing fine. After our rest, we continued on.

We were now over two hours into our journey. The trail had become steeper, and we had to climb over several fallen trees.

"I wonder how far we go before we see the falls," Michael said. He was one of the youngest members of our hikers, and seemed to be getting tired of going downhill.

We soon found a sign, but it announced "Multnomah Falls 9 miles."

What? We had been walking for over 2 hours now, and we were still 9 miles away from our destination? Incredible! Pete and Shirley would be at the bottom of the mountain, waiting for us, and we had a long way to go. We had no way to reach them, as this was 1980, long before we carried cell phones.

An hour and a half later, we finally reached another sign. This one announced the falls as 2 miles away. At least, we were getting closer. We rested for a time, but hoped for this trek to be over soon.

A mile to go, that's what a new sign said. The trail now became very steep, with many switchbacks as we went down the steeper face of the mountain. We were getting very tired by now, and our feet and legs were aching. I kept thinking, "100 yards, turn, 100 yards turn." We were getting closer to the end; the last of the trail, which was by far the steepest, was behind us. We were down! Pete and Shirley were waiting for us.

"Where have you been? We've been waiting for hours!"

"You and your '9 miles!' We walked at least twice that far!" Florence said, as we rested as best as we could on some benches.

We grabbed some cold drinks, and headed to the cars. The next several days, people would look at us and shake their heads. Our legs hurt so badly, we could barely walk. It was especially evident when we got out of the cars.

"Must run in the family," they'd think. "They're all crippled!"

Our trip to Mount St. Helens, 1980

This is not a fish story, but I'm including it here because it occurred during our trip west just after the above story.

After we recovered from our trek down Larch Mountain, we wanted to visit Mount St. Helens. She had blown up on May 18, 1980, and everyone was still watching her closely in August, anticipating another explosion. We decided we would go up the highway as far as we could toward where the observation station had been, to observe first hand the damage and destruction from the explosion.

We headed up the mountain, stopping frequently to take photos of downed trees, logs boiled from the mud, and we were amazed at the magnitude of the damage the explosion had caused. When it blew, an area of about 24 square miles was covered with ash and debris, and the total volume of the deposit was about seven tenths of a cubic mile. Most of St. Helens' former north side became a rubble deposit 17 miles long, averaging 150 feet thick, The slide was thickest a mile below Spirit Lake. The landslide temporarily displaced the waters of the lake to the ridge north of the lake, in a giant wave approximately 600 feet high. This in turn created a 295-foot avalanche of the returning waters and thousands of uprooted trees and stumps.

When she blew, the direct blast zone averaged about eight miles in radius, an area in which virtually everything, natural or artificial, was obliterated or carried away. This zone also has been called the "tree-removal zone". The blast released energy equal to 24 megatons of TNT.

An intermediate zone extended out to distances as far as 19 miles from the volcano, an area in which the flow of mud and boiling water flattened everything in its path. We saw large trees toppled and broken off at the base of the trunk as if they were blades of grass mown by a scythe. This zone was also known as the "tree-down zone".

We ran out of highway when we reached an area where a bridge over the Tuttle River had been washed out by the avalanche of water, steam and mud. We walked down to the river, which was just a small stream, and observed the height of mud on the trees by the river. I estimated the mud line as 35 to 40 feet above the tree roots. We picked up some buckets of dust from the volcano as souvenirs.

While we were wandering around the river, a Forest Service truck pulled up.

"What are you people doing up here?" the ranger asked.

"Just looking at the damage that was done," Shirley replied.

"You shouldn't be here! This thing could explode again at any moment! You need to get out of this area immediately!"

We promptly got back into the car and headed down the mountain again. But we had seen and photographed one of Nature's biggest disasters in modern history.

One day a rather inebriated ice fisherman wandered out on the ice and drilled a hole. As he peered into it, a loud voice from above said, "There are no fish down there."

He walked several yards away, drilled another hole and peered into it. Again, the voice said, "There's no fish down there."

He walked about 50 yards away and drilled a third hole. Once again the voice said, "There's no fish down there."

He looked up into the sky and asked, "God, is that you?"

"No, you idiot," the voice said, "I'm the ice rink manager."

Introduction of salmon into the Great Lakes

How, why, and from where were salmon introduced into the Great Lakes? I will answer that question with this story, some details of which I found on-line at numerous locations, and additional information from my father-in-law, Pete.

In 1964, Lake Michigan's fisheries were in dire straits. The native lake trout had been wiped out in Lake Michigan and Lake Huron. Over fishing and sea lampreys were believed to be the causes, although pollution may have been a factor as well. Whitefish had become endangered, and dead alewives washing up on the beach kept tourists away due to the stench of rotting fish. Something had to change. The man who had to decide what that change would be was Howard Tanner, the state of Michigan's new fisheries chief.

The federal government wanted to bring back lake trout, but Tanner had newer radical ideas. There was surplus of fish eggs up for grabs in the West, but they were coho salmon eggs. The Great Lakes had unsuccessfully planted some of these in tributaries back in 1873. But Tanner's idea was to re-introduce the salmon in 1966, the big change that needed to take place to revive the fishing industry. His plan was to stock the Platte River and Bear Creek with coho salmon smolts, which are young fish that have grown large enough that they turned silver and are ready to head to salt water. Both of these selected streams are tributaries that feed Lake Michigan. Chinook salmon were also selected to be planted in the lake.

My wife's uncle had a brother who was involved with the Department of Natural Resources. Dick Harrison was one of the individuals who brought the young salmon to Illinois, Indiana, Wisconsin and Michigan.

By Labor Day 1967, the fishing industry had exploded in Platte Bay with mature coho salmon, some as large as 20 pounds but averaging closer to 12 pounds. The fish were thriving in the freshwater lakes and fisherman came from miles away to reel them in. Tanner's decision to stock salmon had been in question, as salmon were historically saltwater fish, not freshwater. A Michigan Department of Natural Resources report detailing the immediate years after the salmon were released showed that during September 1967, fall retail sales to sport fisherman jumped by $11.9 million. The numbers continued to increase during the next two years. The salmon had an additional benefit in that they fed on alewives, helping reduce that population, and improving tourism at the beaches.

Chinook and coho salmon are still being stocked in the Great Lakes today. The highest number of coho salmon was stocked in Lake Michigan between 2000 to 2009, while the most Chinook salmon was stocked in Lake Huron during that same time period.

Stocking the steelhead into the Great Lakes was a task undertaken through history by individual states. The steelhead is appreciated by sport fishermen for its appearance, impressive size and strength. In comparison to the rainbow trout, the steelhead is from 2 to 10 times larger in size and weight.

Illinois began stocking the steelhead in harbors and various lakefront areas of Lake Michigan in 1893, just after the Chicago's World Fair. Again, this was met with very poor success until the late 1960s. By the 1970s, sport fishermen were catching fish around Chicago that would migrate from Wisconsin and Michigan, with little stocking effort from the state of Illinois itself.

Indiana began stocking steelhead in 1889, with

the first fish planting in the St. Joseph River. That early program was unsuccessful and officials did not try it again until 1968, with only minimal success. They had found that, like the other early stocking programs, the salmon had difficulty adjusting to the colder water, especially during the winter. In 1971, Indiana began to experiment with a Wisconsin strain of steelhead called the Skamania. They finally began to see some promise. This strain seemed strong enough to handle the winter climate and by 1982, Indiana claimed a victory. The Skamania program is still strong today, and continues to draw fishermen from across the U.S.

Michigan's steelhead history began in 1876 and was continued since then somewhat successfully. The program included both releasing wild fish into the AuSable River with fish from Oregon and breeding them in a hatchery. An updated program began in 1966. Fish populations have been on the increase. Today, the Little Manistee River is the primary source of steelhead eggs in Michigan, enough that they can sell eggs to hatcheries in other states. Meanwhile, lake trout were brought in and stocked once again in Lake Michigan.

Wisconsin's steelhead program began in 1884 but the program didn't really get established until 1963. Twenty years later, Wisconsin selected three strains of the steelhead to stock, which have since thrived in natural reproduction.

Standing at the edge of the lake, a man saw a woman flailing about in the deep water. He couldn't swim, so he started screaming for help.

A trout fisherman ran up.

"My wife is drowning and I can't swim. Please save her. I will give you a hundred dollars."

The fisherman dove into the water, and in ten powerful strokes, he reached the woman. He put his arm around her and swam back to shore. Depositing her at the feet of the man, the fisherman said, "Okay, where's my hundred dollars?"

The embarrassed man said, "Look, when I saw her going down for the third time, I thought it was my wife. But this woman is my mother-in-law."

The fisherman reached into his pocket and said, "Just my luck. How much do I owe you?"

Two guys are talking about fishing. One said to the other, "I am NEVER going to take my wife fishing with me again!"

"That bad, huh"

"She did everything wrong! She talked too much, she made the boat rock constantly, she tried to stand up in the boat, she baited the hook wrong and she used the wrong lures. But WORST of all, she caught more fish than me!"

##

It is now my pleasure to introduce Mr. Gary Stanford. He brings several fishy stories to share.

A fishy tale, and other lines of crappies

My earliest memories of vacations centered around water, lakes, and fishing! My parents had a system for allocating their finances; the envelope system. Each payday, money for utilities, water, and telephone bills went into individual envelopes. Money for food had its own envelope. Money for clothing went into a separate envelope, and money for a vacation had its own envelope.

My first vacation memory, which would have been about 1954, was going to a place in Michigan called "Kate's Lake." I'm not sure if that was the real name of the lake, or if Kate owned the resort or cottages where we stayed. There was a long wooden pier on which we could run and jump into the lake, which was waist deep at that point on a seven-year-old boy. I don't remember fishing there, but we may have. Dad had a boat motor he had borrowed for the trip, but I don't remember us using it as a family. Dad may have used it for fishing.

Two years later, in 1956, our family, which consisted of me, my younger brother, and our mom and dad, who was a fireman, joined two other firemen and their families on a "fishing" vacation on West Gun Lake, Michigan. My best friend, Chuck, son of one of the other families, and I were planning on having the best time being on vacation together. Chuck's father was taking his boat, which he named "the Brokus."

Once we got to the lake, my father, Chuck's father, and Mr. Anderson all went fishing in the big boat. Chuck and I, after much persuading from our mothers, were allowed to use a smaller rowboat, with our own motor. Dad gave me all the rules;

    1. Stay seated in the boat when you start the motor.
    2. Do not stand up in the boat.
    3. Pay attention to where you are on the lake.
    4. No fooling around when you are in the boat.

Once these rules were given, they were to be followed **explicitly**.

We spent the day swimming, boating, fishing and cooking outdoors (grilling was just catching on). That was the summer I learned how to clean fish. I could clean fish with the best of them, but don't expect me to eat them after I cleaned them. No, sir, not gonna happen; I'm not eating THOSE fish!. While the rest of the family had a fish fry, I had a peanut butter sandwich.

One day during this vacation, Dad decided our family would be going on a boat ride across the lake. Chuck and his father had taken "the Brokus" out to fish, so that left us with our little minnow-of-a-boat and motor to go cruising. The four of us climbed into the boat, with me sitting in the bow, Mom and my brother, Rick, sat on the middle seat, and Dad sat on the rear seat so he could operate the motor and steer the boat. It was a beautiful day, with bright sun and beautiful blue sky. The lake water was clear and reflected the sky and a few passing marshmallow clouds. Dad cut the motor, and we just drifted, listening to the silence on the lake broken only by the call of a loon. Time came to head back into shore and dinner at our cottage, so Dad began pulling the cord on the motor. But, instead of the expected *varoom* and *purr*, he heard *plup* and nothing more.

Two more pulls of the cord - three more pulls. Nothing. Standing up in the boat, Dad got a better grip of the cord and gave it one heck of a pull. But, instead of it starting, the motor bucked, sending my father over the side of the boat, and into the lake. Dad went under, and was out of our sight for only about eight seconds, but in that time, our mother said, "Whatever you do, do NOT laugh at your father. Be quiet, and don't even smile!"

First, one hand, followed by another, came out of the lake and grabbed at the boat. With a mighty lunge, as if he was being propelled by some unseen underwater hand, my father reentered the boat. The first words out of his mouth were, "That's why you are NOT to stand up in the boat when starting the motor!"

I think it was my brother who began snickering, followed by laughter from our mother. I was too afraid to laugh, although I was howling on the inside!

A fishing cabin in Wisconsin

My parents purchased a summer cottage on a lake in Wisconsin some years later, and traveled north as often as they could get away in the summer months. My family and brother Rick's family used it also as our children grew up.

One summer, my family and my parents were vacationing together at the lake. My son, Jason, who was maybe 6 or 7 at the time, and Grandpa went out in the boat fishing on the lake. They were gone nearly five hours, and we had begun to worry, when finally they returned.

"What have you been doing out there so long?" Grandma asked.

"We were fishing," announced Jason proudly, "and I peed in a can."

We saw that they had caught a nice mess of fish, bluegill, sunfish, a few perch, and some crappie, as Grandpa unloaded the boat.

"Who caught the most fish?" was the next question.

"_{He caught them all!}" muttered Grandpa under his breath.

"What was that?" I asked. "I didn't hear you."

"He caught them all!" Grandpa repeated, only slightly louder.

"What? Speak up. We still didn't hear you," I chuckled.

"He caught them all! I didn't catch anything!" Grandpa sadly announced.

We all had a good laugh, congratulated Jason on his good day, and teased my Dad for the rest of the trip.

A closing note from John & Gary

A person who enjoys fishing usually is a person who enjoys nature. When you are sitting on a lake, or by the shore of a river or pond, you cannot help but observe your surroundings. The flora and fauna around you certainly catch your attention as you wait for a nibble on your bait. The beauty and serenity of your surroundings grab you and calm you. The sounds of the water lapping at the shore or the side of your boat, or the sounds of a river, stream or waterfall has a special calming effect on a person. Birds calling from the trees, and the wind gently blowing through the limb add to the feeling that everything is right with the world. A fisherman learns to appreciate God's creations, whether observing a beautiful landscape, or watching a tiny ant carry a seed to its anthill; one cannot deny that there was an unseen hand working to create this wonderful masterpiece of a planet we call home.

We hope you have enjoyed these stories. Thank you for reading them.

www.ingramcontent.com/pod-product-compliance
Lightning Source LLC
Chambersburg PA
CBHW050444010526
44118CB00013B/1676